MYCOEPITHALAMIA

Mushroom Wedding Poems

Art Goodtimes
and Britt A. Bunyard, Editors

The FUNGI Press

Copyright ©2016

All rights reserved. Printed in the United States of America. No part of this book may be used, reproduced, or distributed, in any manner whatsoever without prior written permission, except in the case of reprints in the context of reviews.

The FUNGI Press
P.O. Box 780 • Moorpark, CA 93020 USA
fungimag.com

ISBN-10: 0-692-75627-2
ISBN-13: 978-0-692-75627-0

ATTENTION: SCHOOLS AND BUSINESSES
This publication is available at quantity discounts with bulk purchase for educational, business, or sales promotional use. For more information, please e-mail: fungimag@gmail.com.

FRONT COVER: The "Blushing Bride Amanita,"
Amanita novinupta. Photo courtesy of A. Rockefeller.

BACK COVER: *Amanita novinupta*.
Photo courtesy of B. Bunyard.

ILLUSTRATIONS: Aaron "inkling" Cruz Garcia

PRODUCTION EDITOR: Jan Hammond

Printed in U.S.A.

Introduction

Welcome to the marriage of heaven and earth, as Andy Weil would say. We are celebrating the fungal universe in all its sizes, shapes, uses, cults, controversies and philosophies – from myco-remediation of forest clearcuts and oil spills to the gustatory delights of myco-culinary expertise, from Nobel Prize speakers to ecstatic marching bands, from lumpers to splitters, from medicinal potions to entheogenic speculations.

There's a lovely Way of the Mountain chant that goes: "Give thanks to the Earth Mother, Give thanks to the Father Sun, Give thanks to the Shrooms around us, where the Mother and the Father are one."

To wed is to join together, and Britt Bunyard of *Fungi* magazine and Art Goodtimes of the Telluride Mushroom Festival have linked up to offer you poems from the Telluride Institute's Talking Gourds Program, poems that have appeared or will appear in *Fungi*, and poems that were originally performed at the Festival.

Shroomfest, as some of us like to call it, is a serious citizen-science conference, symposium, workshop, and convocation in which parades, poetry and performance have not been strangers. Many poets have read on the mushroom stage before talks by such luminaries as Gary Lincoff, Dr. Weil, Paul Stamets, Laura Huxley, Sasha Shulgin, Joan Halifax, Terence McKenna, Dolores LaChapelle, Ralph Abraham, and Lynn Margulis.

This first issue honors the Salzmans and all the Fungophiles who brought this three-decade tradition to Telluride.

ii

We have arranged the poems we bring you into three categories: Fungi, the Brides; Fungophiles, the Grooms; and Mycelial Mind as the wedding bed, where Sappho would have us "Raise high the roofbeams." How we see, how we feel, how we experience mushrooms, and how that entanglement across kindoms (sic) plays out in people's lives gives this anthology the widest possible scope of inquiry.

As for any good American verse product, robust enough to follow in the ways of Whitman and Dickinson, Cardenal and Harjo, we have aimed for a diversity of voices rather than a uniformity of value. This is the kind of volume to plant beside your pillow, and harvest slowly over time. Especially during those long winter months when neither morels nor pfifferlings appear in one's basket.

Come join in the lyric sporulation.

Shroompa
Cloud Acre
$2^5$016 (New World Calendar)

Publisher's Note

I am very proud of this first poetry offering by The FUNGI Press. Tremendous thanks go to all the authors who have contributed to this project. Special thanks goes to Art Goodtimes for his genius and hard work in pulling together so many talented writers for a common cause: the celebration of fungi! I first met Art during my first year at the Telluride Mushroom Festival. For those who have not yet been, this is the mushroom event of the year. Mushroom Fest is "a celebration of all things mushroom" and features lectures and performances, the likes of which you will not see at any other mycological event—academic, amateur, or otherwise. The poetry at the Festival is one of the facets that I have come to enjoy most.

Our mycological journal had been in print only a few years, celebrating "all things fungal," when Art offered to take on the role as editor of poetry. His contribution to FUNGI has been tremendous. Poetry and essays by award-winning writers, along with our stunning photography, technical as well as nontechnical articles, and regular features are what set FUNGI magazine apart from all other mycological journals out there.

Come to Telluride in August. If the monsoon rains have been generous—and they usually are—you will see the achingly beautiful mountains there carpeted in mushrooms. The forayers will be filling baskets and sharing tales (along with cooking tips). And along Colorado Ave you will hear Art's voice booming out: "We ... love ... mushrooms!"

B A B
2016

Table of Contents

Fungi - The Brides
(poems talking about specific mushrooms)

It's Laughable	2
Il Porcino	3
Boletus Coitus	4
Cloud Acre Nursery Rhyme	6
Home	7
Boleti	8
Aware	9
Chanterelles	10
The Art of Mycophagy	11
Short Season	12
The Art of Getting Lost	13
The Hunt	18
False Chanterelles	20
Chinook and Chanterelle	22
Chamber Mushroom Music	23
Root to Hyphal Rootlet	24
Morels	25
After Many Attempts	26
Good Morning	27
Highway 26	28

Ojo de Dios	30
Crimini	32
Shaggy Mane	33
Inky Caps	34
Hawks' Wings	36
Touching	37
Fungophobia	38
Mushroom	40
Shameless	41
Chaga	42
Iron County	43
The Kingdom of Ignorance	44
Dark Ages	46
Shroom	48
Awakened at Paradise Point	50
Entheogens Take You Away	53
Mushroom Beach	54
Ode to Psilocybe	55

Fungophiles - The Grooms
(poems talking about Telluride's love of and lovers of mushrooms)

Prayer for the Great Shroom	58
John Cage, 1989 Mushroom Festival	63
Way of the Dance	64

Epithalamium Perfecti 65

Remembering Karen Adams 66

Foray 68

Carter Norris 69

Passing the Cabin at Log Corral Creek 70

Camels Garden 72

To Pick Proper 74

Mycosexillogically Chocoluscious 77

Mushrooms 78

Mycelial Mind - The Wedding Bed
(mushrooms as metaphors in lyric musings)

Mushrooms 82

The Risen 83

Εδειν Εστι Ποειν (Edein Esti Poein) 84

Champignon 86

Mushroom 87

Whispering 88

Expiation 89

Soiled Barbie 90

Foray	92
Walk Slowly	93
Absorbed	95
Of Breasts and Mushrooms	96
Опята (Opjata)	98
The Mushroom	100
Fruiting Bodies	101
Center of the Paradox	102
Spent Mushroom's Lament	104
Of Sadness	105
Mushroom Has Landed	106
Autumn In Five Parts	108
Cause and Effect	111
Siempre Cantando Flowers & Shrooms	112
Everyone Has More Rules Than I Do	114
Stony Road	115
The Uses Of Speech	116
Myco-Solstice	118
Hard (Mushroom)	119
Mycelial Mind	120
Author Bios and Acknowledgments	122

Fungi - *The Brides*

It's Laughable

So easy sometimes
to forget how to be alive,
and then, walking the edges
of the spruce forest,
we come across in the duff
not just the brown cap
of *Boletus edulis* but
that whatever it is
that we have forgotten,
simple and humble and miraculous,
it was there all along,
not really hiding,
just waiting for us
to find it.

    Rosemerry Wahtola Trommer

Il Porcino

I'll never forget the taste
Of your brow,
The subtle hints of magic,
Of dark color,
Hidden in the most unassuming of places—
tucked under, peeking out of,
the strands surrounding you.

Oh ancient animal of the forest,
you give us such succulent treasures,
a richness that cannot be replicated.

Elle Masaracchia

Boletus Coitus

now that the rains are here
I look for you every morning
your shiny head
hard, ready, poking out
from earthy covers
shrouded in moist greening hair

how I want you
virile king
mycelial talons unbuckling my dreams
sliding off each night
slippery, wet feet
diving into hunt

I carry my box
open, ready, a crevasse
for your long white flesh

the many faces of you
invite, coax with scent
thread me through naked blue and fallen golds
past deer bones, deserted beer cans
teasing with jacks and agarics
every sexy spotted red nub
making me want you more

there, right there
here
jutting like a bull pine
ripe, thick, ready
you dance me to you
I squeal, you wait
a fixed flower
microscopic pulses
patient as I coo
pull you into my world
lips moist
fire hot
ready

Blake More

Cloud Acre
Nursery Rhyme

One porcino
Two porcini
Three potato four

You kiss my spud
& I'll kiss
your spore

Art Goodtimes

Home
– for Rio

When you carry all your own water into a house,
letting it run free, even to wash hands seems almost

sinful. 'Cepting, I don't believe in sin. But I do believe
genuflect & prostrate at the altar of first mistakes. Do

humbly confess & on occasion apologize, as well as
give thanks for improvements. Embracing what's done

Whether regretted or held up to the light. People
parading Boletes & Amanitas up Colorado Ave.

Or Pops filing for fungal divorce. Push comes to
shove, my cloud whirls around a wind of aspen

Chapbooks. Bed. Stove. Friends & offspring
who-can-accept-what-I-regret, as well as

what-I-champion. Rituals. Familiars – all the
intimates & rorschachs of interior life. Call home

the place where I find myself, holding hands
with Rainbows. Pissing on a Bush. Laid out flat

on my back in the quackgrass looking up &
laughing at the Universe TV of fellow stars

Art Goodtimes

Boleti

Argentum atque aurum facile est laenamque
togamque
mittere: boletos mittere difficile est.

Mushrooms

It's easy to send silver, or gold, or a nice cloak, or
a toga: but mushrooms are difficult to part with.

Martial
tr. Art Beck

[Trans. Note: This is from Martial's collection, Xenia, "gift tags," to accompany Saturnalia food presents. These and the similar Apophereta are the only Martial poems with titles.
Martial Book XIII ("Xenia") #48]

[Ed. Note: "Boletus, Boleti, Boletos" was the Latin name for what American fungophiles and modern day Italians know as Amanita caesarea – a choice edible species but one of the few among a genus famous for Death Caps and Destroying Angels]

Aware

Kamikaze deer
rams the Dodge van
Torpedoes our campout lark

And bad luck, the dent's
Irreversible, having spaced
the Geico bill this month

Still, we find shrooms in the woods
my son & I. Voluptuous boletes
& goth hawkwings fry on the fire

Art Goodtimes

Chanterelles

Up in the pines near fallen logs
we find them clustered, heaved up through
needled earth, or under leaves,
bright yellow, and if we look close,
with scalloped caps like lilies have.

A little song to frighten ghosts?
Late summer dance around a tree?
Two days after a thunderstorm
mycophagists have no fears to fend.

I gather them from soft, black beds
cutting at each moss-buried base,
then place each gently in a bag
to take home. I can almost taste
the buttery dish they'll make for us.

Their gold rubs off on my fingers.

                  Beth Paulson

The Art of Mycophagy

In Camden-by-the-Sea, Valli's Greg
hunts chanterelles by gravesites
in the small veiled hours after rain.
Like many, his passion nearly killed him once.
Now, he reaches for a thick knife,
slices cap from stalk,
waits til the gills let go in death,
reads the spores like tea leaves,
and only then lets the flesh
pass between his lips.
A gallery of his conquests lines the walls.
A ghostly filigree traces
each small sphere's identity,
beguiling whether wholesome or not.

Erin Robertson

Short Season

Mother and daughter
in the Lizard Head Wilderness,
on their knees picking chanterelles.
It will be late before they return.
What is more priceless than a heavy
basket of mushrooms.
I keep out of sight because
I would be frightening.

        Peter Waldor

The Art of Getting Lost
– for George Sibley

Okay, so there's this Telluride hippie
hitchhiking up to Junction
Long hair. Backpack.

Suddenly a Winnebago
pulls up with Texas plates
& the tinted window rolls down.

"Howdy, pilgrim!
Could you point me the way
to the nearest wilderness mall
parking lot?"

And our hippie says,
"Hey, man – get lost!"

But I say, before *you* lose it
look closely, because
it's not so much *you* losing it
as the place
that takes you away.

It's slickrock deer trail thick with juniper
takes you away.
It's Mancos shale wild strawberry
avalanche chute...
And suddenly *όλλα καλά*

πάντα ρει
you're just another
neopagan zenmother Budada.

Mastering pandemonium.
Toking pure chaos.

Cougar in the headlights
takes you away.
Morning chanterelles
in a spruce-fir meadow.

Or maybe
it's at a table over breakfast
where some resort-town waitron
Venus Kali clone
takes you away.

And falling in love
you lose it.

Take Luna in the mushrooms & quackgrass.
Rolling in it on Sheep Mountain
that first green-eyed summer.

Or take that infamous hike we took
to the San Miguel Canyon petroglyph
that scribed a hoop in the earth
& led us back to our beginnings.

Remember

you can't lose
what you haven't found.

Double rainbow on Dallas Divide.
Clambering hands & knees up Lone Cone scree.
Uncompahgre's Tabeguache pine scratched by bear.

Getting so lost
you find yourself.

Toad kachina grotto vision
on Nuvatik-ya-ovi
the San Francisco Peaks
[whisper]

Big Sur hot spring
crotch-of-the-redwood
full moon pool
[speak]

Pacific Rim combers
in a Salt Point storm
slamming down fists
takes you away.
[shout]

Letting go
enough
not to panic

but to play it like a tune
whistled & hummed
as a hymn to the Mother.

Easy bro,
Haleakala's charm
takes you away.
Yo, eating mangos & making love
in the sea cave at Kalalau
takes you away.

This IS
my religion.
I believe in being lost.

Everything I find on the way
esta milagro
& what finds me
I try to field.

Thinking
adventure not predicament.
Chasing chaos
just as much as calm.

The only straight lines in the headwaters
are the rifle's scope
& the map's compass.

So, scram pathfinders.
Surveyors.
Engineers.

Gimme the loon's zigzag walk.

Let me lose it.
I know how to use it.

Art Goodtimes

The Hunt

I am 11 years old
Mother Mary is teaching me
to "hunt" mushrooms
She is holy the holiest
of all Marys
It is a sacred hunt
and we must be sacred
like Diana the huntress
only earthier
dirtier
quieter
softer
respecting what we hunt worshipping
the hunt peaks
silently gentle fingers slide
under a damp pile of molding leaves
at the base of a tree
lifting
uncovering
oh holy Mary
teach me about

the tracks the animals make

how to read the animals

by what they leave behind

show me that in the darkest part

of the muskiest forest

there is gold

chanterelles

teach me how to find such magic

buried under death

teach me the tricks

of a deep pan

and butter and garlic

and pure bliss

                Blaize Johnson

False Chanterelles

He said he'd never been mushroom hunting
So we went
Slipping thru pine needle canals
between islands of moss
Supersaturated green
Eyes moving to port and starboard
A lighthouse beacon
On the watch for that
Very special something
Very special someone
And then
Gold
Tingles up my spine
Running forward to investigate
A brilliant orange on forest floor
I grab
Hold to nose
"What did you find?" he asks
Suddenly there at my shoulder
But something is not right
It smells too clean and indistinct
The thick pungent scent of ripe
apricots nowhere to be found

An imposter, fool's gold
My heart sinks
I turn, eyes meeting eyes
I avert
Notice how his beard is too cleanly trimmed
His uncalloused hands seem out of place here
I realize vaguely that he has told a joke
I laugh politely
And we head back
Eyes still scanning to port and starboard
But deep in the ocean of my mind
Plates collide
Forming chaotic ridges
Like the jaunty gills of the true chanterelle
And welling up at my center
A hot orange magma
Burning away all that is false
And leaving behind
A chance
The hope to taste the true tomorrow

Elissa Dickson

Chinook and Chanterelle

What gifts these are
from river and woods. These
coral ones, muscled strumpets, plucked
from the fishers' nets
where the shrunken runs
still shine. And these
golden ones, fluted trumpets, pinched
from the forest floor
where the second-growth hemlocks
still stand. Surely—
we are unworthy of such as these!

But if enjoyment of succulent flesh
is any mitigation, if the tongue's
fierce possession of taste
can be extenuation, if the way
we chew and praise and slurp and swallow
and—say it—worship this fin and stipe,
these silver scales and meaty caps,
can sing the hard shimmer
in the stream can cry the soft glimmer
on the mossy floor can save us—
if these gestures make
any difference whatsoever, well,
then maybe we deserve them
after all.
    Robert Michael Pyle

Chamber Mushroom Music

Chanterelles simmer
in a pan of butter, garlic
diced walla wallas

I stand by the stove
Chef. Conductor

Remembering the Mozart
of her morning strings
sizzling beneath me

& the hot sighs
of our mingled oils

Art Goodtimes

Root to Hyphal Rootlet

Needles fall to the forest floor
erase old foot-trails and form
a thick rusty brown nest
for new orange chanterelles
tiny caps webbed to trees
root to hyphal rootlet.

Maze of woods dims the light
thickets of berry vines muffle
outside noise, the forest
shields us from intrusion
the mushroom-hunter
his clanging pail.

No sound except an owl perching
beetle burrowing into bark
these breaths of air
we who have no place but here.

    Henri Bensussen

Morels

Morchella lift convoluted intentions on
stems clean and hollow as bird bones,
make mazes for May's aradids, scrunch
gnomed caps up through their elm leaf-
littered forest haunts, peeking, furtive,

while

we search, big-eyed, compare what we
see among ground debris with patterns
impressed on the complex paths of our
brains, correlate ridges, pits, wrinkled
edges, shapes recalled in April dreams.

Roy J. Beckemeyer

After Many Attempts

Just because it wasn't here yesterday
doesn't mean it won't be here today.
Some things arrive only in their own time.
Just because I am talking about morels
doesn't mean I'm not talking about love.
And here it is, golden and misshapen,
something I step over once before discovering.
I mean, isn't it wonderful when sometimes
we choose to show up and then, well,
it's not really an accident, is it,
that we find ourselves
with our hands, our hearts so full.

                  Rosemerry Wahtola Trommer

Good Morning

beside him holding his arm
as he took his last breath
at the VA

Palo Alto near Mountain View
high fogs
reincarnate into blue

as they often do
on the Peninsula
in the San Andreas dawn

especially in a dry year
Big Sur
an inferno of crown fires

promising next spring's morels
Dad dead at first light
gaunt & beautiful

Art Goodtimes

Highway 26

I like the way the road
curves toward the coast, past
the white birch forest, 26 West
I can't get lost there's nowhere else to go.

At the only café in Elmira
they brag about Marionberry pie
and hot coffee on their grease-splattered menu,
truckers and tourists, their only customers.

We stop for mushrooms
at the farm stand
that sell for several dollars
less a pound than in the gourmet stores.

I gently brush the woods-earth
that clings to their gills
lobster,
matsutake,
morels,
crimini,
chicken of the woods,

chanterelles,
People have been shot
over mushroom rights,
they tell us when I buy a jar of honey
from the long-haired man
he winks at me tucks an extra jar
of Forest Grove clover
into my bag

Back home,
we sauté the mushrooms
with garlic and sweet butter
their caps caramelize
the garlic burns.

                    Pat Kennelly

Ojo de Dios

We're in the kitchen, bien
sur, barefoot, we're wearing the soft grey sweats
you, the bottoms, and me,

on saute duty, butter melting,
a swirl of gold,
in the copper pan bought
at the market outside Tangiers,
from that Bedouin woman, yes?
her dark eyes &
bangles of silver coined from moonlight -

light on every side.
We gleam like that today.

Steller jays on the feeder,
Satie in stereo,

burner's on, ready for shallots, slender slices of
crimini mushrooms,
fresh tomatoes and hence basil, gruyere...
love and breakfast needing always cheese.

Ready for

scones about to come out of the oven, raspberry jam

remember the day we picked all those berries up in
La Cueva,
wildflowers in full tilt, Echinacea and foxglove? -

Green tea in the pot ready to pour,
and us,
ready for anything.

Judyth Hill

Crimini

These fruits of Hades
spring up for the connoisseur
who combs the grounds
as he pleases,
hands finding pleasures
to tease the palate: stem, cap, gill. Hades'
overnight treasures.

                Judith Skillman

Shaggy Mane

Shy waterfall.
Popped rivet.
Light pole.
I don't wait
for my sons
to cut but cut
on my own--
the greed
of the mushroom
hunter.
It deliquesces
before they arrive.
Shaggy Mane,
had I sought
enlightenment
instead of mushrooms
we would have
held hands
around you
and whispered
the Hopi prayer
and for the seventh
direction, the heart,
said nothing at all.
Shaggy Mane,
dark milk dream
of a better world,
forgive me for not
listening to you.
Shaggy Mane.

Peter Waldor

Inky Caps
– for Jimbo & CarolAnne

White heads poke through
the grass along the paved blacktop
on my way down to his Beckett Point
beach house on Discovery Bay
They catch my motor eye

I pull over & back up
Mushrooms! *Coprinus
comatus* – a favorite edible
from Land's End days
with San Fran Mycological

Savory but short-lived
Have to be cooked
within the hour & eaten
Or white flesh discolors
pink, turns obsidian

& dissolves into an inky goo
No lollygagging waxpaper
field cleaning basket stroll
ritual – with
a honeymoon in the fridge

So I grab a fist-full
& race 'em to Jimbo's stove
to sauté &, soon, consume
Delicious! Nutritious!
They may look fragile

but we're talking
slo-mo battering rams
Able to lift sidewalk concrete
in a single growth spurt
Bless their wayside

fruiting bodies
& gratitude to Ish Nation's
gift of place
Pillar of hyphae!
Choice edible in a ditch!

Art Goodtimes

Hawks' Wings

Though cool and soft
the mushroom is volcanic--
it erupts and pushes
dirt into a mound,
here hawks' wings,
their Frankenstein
tops shining.
Two boys stoop
and cut far down as they can.
They handle the mushrooms
more gently than boys
handle things, trimming
the worms which fall
in the discarded flesh,
still enough to nourish
them into damsel flies.
The boys refuse to fold
their knives, walking away
under the ancient canopy
with hawks' wings in one hand
and blades in the other.

Peter Waldor

Touching

This young cat's fur, ghost strands, long,
chaotic silken, not short, smooth, orderly
like the coarse hair on her tortoiseshell elder.
I'm lucky, I think, to be here, away from war.

In Ashkalon or Gaza, I'd be stroking a daughter's
sunken shoulders, warming her slumped head,
combing the unkempt hair not yet torn,
out of agony for those she's lost.

The kitten turns her head like an owlet,
pushing her ears into my palm, ears thin–
pliant as oyster mushrooms. I massage them
warm between forefinger and thumb.

The inestimable, lucky luxury of peace:
warm bed, purring cats, intact quiet room.

Janet B. Eigner

Fungophobia

I've always been terrified of wild mushrooms,
      never tempted to eat them,
      sure of a slow, painful death,
      or at the very least, projectile vomiting.

But then Art arrived at our house
      with two paper bags from the farmers market.

A charismatic presence with his
      huge beard, huge voice,
      huge enthusiasm for all things fungophilic,
      Art opened the bags and proudly displayed:
           Cauliflower Mushrooms
           Winter Chanterelles
           Lion's Mane.

He soon had us intoning:
      Sparassis
      Hericium
      Craterellus,
      rolling the names around on our tongues,
      admiring the folded shapes,
      touching the pliant skins.

But not satisfied with lip service from his converts,
    this wild priest advanced to the kitchen
    calling for butter and a pan.

Soon there were glasses of wine,
    and small plates with fragrant morsels
    offered up by Art.

I took a deep breath -
    and surrendered.
The tastes were as exotic and delicious
as the names.

At least I knew if I died now I would be
among friends.
    And hadn't Art said there's only a couple of
    kinds that'd kill you.

        Carol Anne Modena

Mushroom

Cool as water,
Plucked of stem,
It floats in my two hands
Like some sea thing
Blind and twisted up
From the refrigerated dark.
Velvet nuzzle nose,
It stains my fingers
Like tea leaves,
Like wet earth.
If I touch too hard,
It breaks,
Flings off
Its feathered gills
Fine as confetti.

O Sea Thing!
O Portabella!
Skulking into the night
Like your poisoned cousins.
Against my tongue,
Above the sizzling skillet,
You are all white trout
And rubbery tire,
Forgotten sometimes,
Forbidden
Never.

Kathryn Winograd

Shameless

Page 178 of **Exotic Mushrooms**
serves up Plate 146, and on this plate
rests *Phallus impudicus*, a steamy
sprout of a mushroom that looks like
you understand more Latin than you thought.
Plate 146 also stipulates, *Not Edible*,
a warning included for the soft-headed,
those who demand everything and want it
all spelled out. I might have penciled in
my own words but I tried that once
in the third grade before a stiff ruler
bruised my knuckles—wielded by a nun,
Sister Gabriel, who guarded the pure
white page, archangel at the gates of desire.
By fifth grade our textbooks contained
not only hastily written words but sketches too,
and some of them surprising for their
anatomical correctness. Fifth graders knew
so much more than exams could ever assess,
but opening our books back then
we had no way to understand character or
the dark soil from which it so suddenly appeared.

David Feela

Chaga

Poise.
Winter rests her sleeping head.
Recumbent in her latent embrace,
You thrive.
Tenuous bark of Birch
Glides into the abyss,
And you arc born as a sable
Light.
You are the last charcoal of nature's whip
A tinder fungus to be used
When heat is no longer enough
To rouse
Even the most broken of
Souls.

Megan Wesko

Iron County

> Said to be the largest and oldest living object
> on earth, covers 38 acres and weighs
> as much as 220,000 pounds.

Beneath my feet, beneath yours,
beneath the feet of trees, of beetles.
thrives the ever entrenching fungus:
The Mother, relentless as lava,
throwing up her fluted sentries
like spikes anchoring her to Earth's crust.

Larger than the forest, than the puny
false borders of states, she munches
steadily forward through the dead wings
of crawlers and collapsing leaves;
and the mushrooms pop pop
up through the mulch
pop pop pop through leaf blankets
and the green tides of moss.

Her little soldiers, the children
of The Mother are rising
across forest floors, along
dry stream beds and behind you,
when you are not looking, they are rising
and signing to each other that
The Mother is on the move.

                CB Follett

The Kingdom of Ignorance

Armillaria bulbosa,
a common mushroom, can grow
larger than a blue whale.
One was found in Minnesota
whose cytoplasm spans
thirty-seven acres underground.
It weighs fifteen-hundred tons
and is as many years old.
No other mushroom
dares to grow in its realm.
Let us toast to invisible spores
extending the Kingdom of Fungi.
And across the savanna
elephants signal each other
in sounds too low for human ears.
They tell about water, poachers,
or to come to the funeral
of one of their fallen.
Oh, the boulder aflame
with migrating Monarch butterflies,
the salmon's return
to the scent of its spawning,

the data dance of bumblebees,
the vastness of *armillaria bulbosa*.
We could trek to Minnesota
to honor this mushroom monarch,
then on to the boundless domain
of Siberian tundra
claimed by a single slime mold.
Here's to fungal reigns
unmapped and unexplained.
Praise be to mold
on the food that we hoard,
to the shaved heads of ringworm,
to stinky feet and itchy crotch.
And to the universe of scents,
of which the common dog
is a scholar.
Here's to the solemn procession
of elephants
and to our ignorance
and awe.

                Donald Levering

Dark Ages
– for Christian Raisch

Only dark
because the power sands
of the Holy Roman Empire
had run out

& the Vatican's papal
bulls & bullies
no longer trampled
the town squares

Instead, imagine ancient
rituals with local headmen
& wise woman healers
running the show

Knowledge wasn't
locked up in tabernacles
Mimes & minstrels
abounded

The game had slipped out
of the hands of
bishops & knights
It was a dangerous time

And exciting. Like today
With culture seeping
underground
& sprouting up

not in buttressed monastic
libraries but in village
huts & hearths
The pagan flowering of

psilocybes. Polypores
Destroying angels
Roses gone wild & lilies
where you'd expect a bog

Mead was made
for religion not revelry
& beer crafted in the ferment of
the hallucinatory

When the Church's red hats
regained control
they burnt the witches
& dubbed the ages dark

On the altar of history
truth's beeswax candles
guttered to a halt
& flashed out

And what light there was
only comes down to us now
through the horribly stained
glass of heresies

Art Goodtimes

Shroom

Such a fast and funny word
for you,
so stealthy, silent.
I do not know your secret name,
just those we give you—
silly sounds
you would not put upon yourself, your kind.

Green-headed Jelly Club
White Dunce Cap
Fuzzy Foot and
Poison Pie,
Destroying Angel
Witch's Hat.
And some of you we label slimes
with gills descending,
woody stalk.
Phallus duplicatus

no surprise you lurk around
wet stumps
dark dirt
until we pluck you
eat you
ecstasy
you sate us
and sometimes
you kill us for it.

Thrust up and out,
erupt
quick spurt
then settle back to brooding
in a puff of silver smoke.

                Lynda La Rocca

Awakened at Paradise Point

1
Sparked by Olympian bolts of lightning,
mushrooms rise
out of earthen beds
of leaves and fecund debris.
Geastrum fornicatum

Rounded bodies arch
pale brown and ripe.
Earth Stars
earthbound
release a galaxy of spores,
breathe silent seeds
into fertile air.

2
He slumps in shadow
amid the rot of pine and oak
wrapped in the shaggy remnants
of a gray, woolen cloak,
large, black cap pulled low.
Strobilomyces strobilaceus

Stalk shriveled
covered with coarse, black scales
Old Man of the Woods
ages,
endures beyond the autumn equinox.

3
A chorus of trumpeters
raises fluted margins to the sky
hollow
brittle and black.
Craterellus fallax

Within their sweet song,
Black Trumpet Chanterelles
sound a warning of dark approach,
herald the fall.

4
Buried beneath a shroud of pine needles
head bowed
body veiled
she pushes upward through forest duff,
rises shining, opalescent
sheathed in white,
ring flaring on her slender neck.
Amanita virosa

Pale and beautiful
Destroying Angel
unfurls fragile wings into autumn light,
lifts mortals through burning flames
to paradise.

Suzanne Marshall

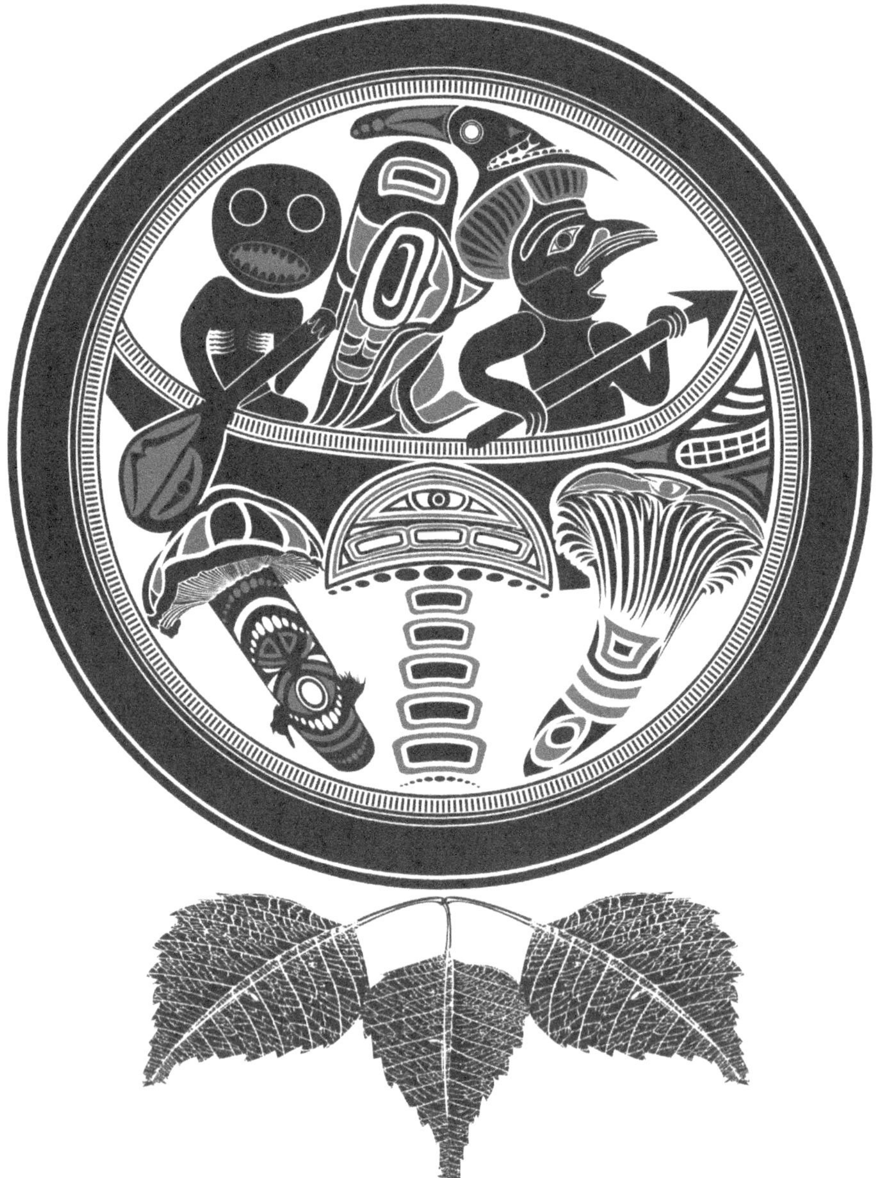

Entheogens Take You Away

What's to wait for?
McRedeye tells
the Red Monk

Sit
like you might never
get up again

Start that singing
inside
some call prayer

& others ayahuasca
Psilocybe
Cannabis sativa

Every chair
in death's waiting room
attaches to a sacred ground

Feel dirt's delerious electricity
feeding the quantum
flowering of

Higg's boletes
chanterelle quarks & whole fields
of hawkwing quasars

Art Goodtimes

Mushroom Beach

Not like that time mushrooms tilted the beach
and the catalog boys walked off a ripped page
asking, what time is it? how much farther is it?
where are we? We just fell down into the trees
bending, laughing low, no, not like that, but
it was a tilting, and walking was difficult.

                Danny Rosen

Ode to Psilocybe

Every spring when raging rainstorms were
followed by warm days and nights, southern style,
proud in manure you grew, *Psilocybe
cubensis*, magic mushroom, bounty of
rich earth, golden crowns rising to greet us—
blessed, harvested, dried, shared with those of like
mind. Our communion, friendships' bitter seal.
Cleansed doors of perception revealed to us
spiders' subtle eggs, infinite worlds, our
hidden inheritance, saffron courage.

It has been years, old friend, since we last met
on my thirtieth birthday, but I swear
I hear you, Maecenas of the pasture,
singing blank verse odes in ebony nights,
calling me to return to damp dark fields,
to pull on my boots, to venture into
meadows wet with yesterday's rain, to turn
four times around before scanning the ground.
To find *there*, by my right foot, another
clarity—a path home at this late hour.

Jeanetta Calhoun Mish

Fungophiles - The Grooms

Prayer for the Great Shroom

Gratitude to Fungi

Gift to the clans
from the powers below ground
The de-composers
Breaking down
strings of amino acids
& fatty woodwind arpeggios

Composting dead trees into creekside
kettledrums. Orchestrating
the grand wheeling
kiva crescendo of
singing
cycling & recycling

Sparked by nature's
spore plugs of regeneration
Edulis
Cibarius
Esculenta

Polypores. Puffballs
Stinkhorns. Earthstars
Corals & Clubs

(Antiphonal)
(Bard:)
In our hearts, minds
stomachs & synapses
so be it...
(The Assembled)
So be it!

And gratitude to the Fungophiles
The Salzmans
Lincoffs
Andrew Weil
Paul Stamets & Dusty Yee
Corbin. Klite. Norris
The Gillmans & the Adamses

Tie-dye locals & suit&tie regulars
And to all us pot-hunting
mountain crazies
jonesing for another foray

Throwbacks to an earlier dawn
Of earth dancers
Soil singers

Not *Homo sapiens* but *Humus ludens*
Hunting & gathering once again
on Lizard Head slopes
& in Sheep Mountain forests
encircling
To-Hell-u-Ride

Playful mud men & mud wymyn
getting down dirty to
dig up stipes

Or
cross-species dressing up
to parade down Colorado Ave.

Swearing fealty
to the sacred
Shroom

(Antiphonal)
(Bard:)
In our hearts, minds
stomachs & synapses
so be it...
(The Assembled)
So be it!

Honor the goddess in all her guises
Be she healing tonic
gourmet treat or
amatoxin hell
for those who pick without respect

And may we all experience
(if just once)
the whiz-bang
berserker inebriation of
amanita muscaria

Yes!
We love Mushrooms!

So raise high the galactic roofbeam
Sasha. Terence.
Dolores LaChapelle

& let us enter
the flavor of xerampolina
The aroma of matsutaki
The ling chi tea of Chinese longevity

Let us bioassay
(at least once)
& join in praise of all entheogens
but particularly cubensis

Entangling us in the power
the glory & the mycelial
warp of black holes
dark matter & death's mystery

(Antiphonal)
(Bard:)
In our hearts, minds
stomachs & synapses
so be it...
(The Assembled)
So be it!

Art Goodtimes

John Cage, 1989 Mushroom Festival

He went in pajamas
at four AM on his foray,
freezing in the Kilpacker Basin's
open meadows and then
the trail dipped into the forest
and the temperature rose
a few degrees because the trees
held heat from the previous day.
Cage noticed the temperature
and guessed the reason,
it was just enough to make him
warm and lucky to be alive
on the earth which glowed.
His friends knew he returned
with no boletes
and no chanterelles,
just one giant
Puff Ball, past its prime.
We know the small ones
have more spores than
there are stars in our galaxy.
But better to call
the spores unlived lives
and call the mountains what
the Utes called them – Shendokas—
rainmakers, the Utes,
before we destroyed them.

Peter Waldor

Way of the Dance

In the gospel according
to Laura Huxley

any day without dance
would be a sin

Any creed be made to
teetertotter, bread & water

& match wits
with pure monkey

Shrooms would have
their own altars

San Pedro
Acid & ayahuasca too

Death would be no island
And we'd all sashay

our way along
arm & arm with ecstasy

Art Goodtimes

Epithalamium Perfecti

Hard not to celebrate
mushrooms today
as much as a marriage

as we come to McMenamins
to witness & bless
this union of Stamets & Griffith

La Dena & Benjamin
joining as fungi do
cap to stipe

to rise as something wholly other
Fruitful bodies
freed of their veils

Raise high the wedding basket
& honor what they've collected
Succulent edibles

The startling medicinals
of a turkey tail miracle
& entheogenic love

May their hyphae
twine amid the roots
of this challenged world

& mycorrhizal
heal & thrive
in all life's rainbow glory

Art Goodtimes

Remembering Karen Adams

Year after year
we'd gather together
our brainy ragtag shroomfest crew

Much like our hunter/gatherer
ancestors – all the scattered bands
meeting for the annual big time

Karen always there,
she who mothered plants for a living
A nurturer by nature

And always
the spark plug armillaria
of the Adams clan

Like the shrooms she loved
to identify, surprises hid
beneath her cap of convention

A kind of cheeky daring
in the face of psilocybes
so frightening to her peers

Hers was an entheogenic appetite
for humor & a goddess's
hunger for love

So now, decomposed
her fruiting body having returned
to the mysterious mycelia

beneath us all, we honor her
& call upon her simple name
to ring our arms around

Art Goodtimes

Foray
A Fungophile's Epithalamium
– for Jason & Anne

It's sunrise
& we are rising with you
in the mists of a new morning

where a new life
will burst out of the dew
& duff

Head like a mushroom
bearing your spore
And joining hands

under the banner of our clan
we'll all march
& dance & make merry

celebrating the wild
& visible fruiting
of unseen ties

that surprise us
with colorful family
Rich lives

Art Goodtimes

Carter Norris

You couldn't help notice
the dapper moustache
as he shook your hand
warmly

Aussie bush hat
Worn one flap up
& one tied down
to earth

To mushrooms

To that inner wild
that he showed
a few of us

amid the daily
muck-a-muck
in which he waded

A make-it-happen
kind of guy

happening now
with us in spirit

Art Goodtimes

Passing the Cabin at Log Corral Creek

Stack a rock & make a cairn
in honor of the late Paul Klite

Plein air impresario of roguish
insights. Bemushroomed Picasso

of impish play. Remember not just
the sleek dome of that capital wit

but his wry mustachio'd grin
Never nasty but sly

Gone the booming voice
The basso profundo of words

that healed, a mind that raced
at the speed of a surgeon's slice

Standing under the *terra infirma*
of this fallen roof in the woods

I can hear his gypsy fiddle
aflame in the subterranean

realms of mycelia & laughter
And growing through the floor

boards I can see the fruiting body
of his life's deep doubletalk

His art's last double take
One perfectly blue columbine

Art Goodtimes

Camels Garden

Three boulders like camels' humps
rise in the mountain forest
blind to the twisting jeep road.
In the shotgun seat
I avoid looking downhill
the open jeep
an invitation to blend
with aspens and blue spruce.

Slipping on shale to master a switchback.
A meadow appears and three
log structures: a fox farm.
Hauled all day by foot and burro pack
to isolation, cold and snow
to roaming and easy breathing.

The distance levels me
with snow-tipped peaks—Wilson,
Lone Cone, Sneffels—and every nerve
becomes giddy sinks like a feather.

The aspen's quiver is not a flinch
but a flexibility of acceptance.
Harebells, Indian paintbrush, mountain
violets succor my gritty eyes.
The snow-cooled breeze peels
my skin to the raw freeing my sex
tingling to every crevice and muscle.

I am surrounded by boundaries
that leave no doubt.
A final sigh and I am released
as the fox farmers were released.

Back in the jeep, down
the other side to search
for new mushrooms among the aspens.
No luck.
It's been a dry summer.

                Gayle Lauradunn

To Pick Proper

There's no way to walk
back across the Bering Straits

No way to deny Columbus his discovery &
slam the gears of the still Roman Empire

in reverse. No way to trade
a remembered chalice for the blade

The Paleolithic's paradise of
partnership cultures is long kaput

Here deep in the heart of the West
one of Patriarchy's last frontiers

romanced as we continue to be
by winter wheat & rye

goat cheese & cow's milk
With our best animal allies

long ago domesticated. Cat
& dog. Ox & camel. Even the horse

at full gallop, clinging with our thighs
is what betrayed the tribe's trust

& accelerated the fatal switch from
hunter-gatherers to herders & rowcroppers
Here on the Rocky Mountain edge of
the ancient inland sea we can

step back into our old ways
as future primitives and augment

the industrial harvest with what
we glean from the forest duff

or roadside ditch. Wild Asparagus
*Coprinus comatus * Boletus rubriceps*

Some of us still hunt what edibles abound
in & around us – our neighbors & nourishment

But, if we do, we ought to observe
the proper etiquette of honor &

thanks. Perhaps just a song. A whisper
on our breath, as we snap the stalk

Cut the green stem of spring low
to the ground so the roots fruit

more & those that follow the way
we go will have stalks galore

In some years maybe three or four
Fruitings. Flowerings. Sprouting bodies

With shrooms it's most important
to field clean * Using a knife

you snip the chanterelle from the earth's
grip: "Sticking it to you, toadstool"

& scrape the clinging dirt. Moss. Bad
spots. Wormy gills. A stipe too tough

to eat (any blemish even) until the flesh
you take is clean. Ready to pop

in the pan without washing – which
kills the delicate flavor of champignon

Most mushrooms really, loaded as they are
with protein & strange alkaloids. The beauty is

those scrapings full of spore help
propagate & spread the fungus & thus

by taking the time to sing & clean each
cap, we keep the patch alive – that

invisible mycelial mat which connects us
rhyzomic immortals, to everything else

Art Goodtimes

Mycosexillogically Chocoluscious

The god-
dess of fungi erotica
& mycosensuality erupts fruitfully
thrusting his stalk erect from the duff
She spreads her gills & his stem penetrates
her flesh She arches her cap & spores rain down
spreading abundant spurts & spirals of love
throughout her everpresent mycelial web
connecting you to me to her
& all sensual &
erotic beings
in the
uni-
verse
Remember
to honor
your-self
with at
least
one
act
of
self
love
today
& may
all of your
connections
bear fruit

Tamara Davis

Mushrooms
– for Pablo & Dusty

Hiking alone up a morning ravine
in the wild Santa Cruz mountains.

Dappled shadows through laurel leaf
& porcupine-thick pine boughs.

Moss-skinned stones splashed with
water whispering its way to the sea.

There! Spotlighted on a bench of sun
one lone parasol of red (*Hygrophorus*

I would learn later). Waxy cap &
stem stunning in its phallic form

& solitary rise, as though springing
full grown from out the brow of

the creek's bank. Miracle of fungal life
& death recycled. A mycelial mystery

that started it all for me – the Way of
the Fungophile. Tracking the hyphae

of chthonic connections from roots
to fruiting bodies. Enzymes to alkaloids.

Ekto/endo mutualism to Terence McKenna's
entheogenic consciousness. Coming to

understand reciprocal appropriation. How
the fungal kindom is affording us

the opportunity now – in the shadow
of the mushroom cloud – to help

heal the planet we as a viral
species have infected. Irradiated.

Baptized & globalized. One
lone shroom. Revealing herself in

nature as the thousand-armed goddess.
Icon. Antidote. Our best hope.

Art Goodtimes

Mycelial Mind - *The Wedding Bed*

Mushrooms

The Anishinaabeg once called it *puhpowee*,
that force
which stirs in secret, lifting leaf mold,
surprising even the serious oaks,
who wake to find at their feet
these new beings, peopling their forest.
All in the damp dark, they come reaching,
sent
summoned
pushed
drawn
with a power so particular, it earns its owns name.

Amber Veverka

The Risen

To speak it is to become it.
Divining the dimensions of a space it has taken
Beneath me
The way it summons by coloring
The air: its edict. And I, servant, humbly
With knife and pan and butter,
Raze and raise the fruiting body.
Divining the dimensions of the space it is taking;
To eat it is to become it.

Haz M. Said

*Εδειν Εστι Ποειν**

– for Katrina Blair & the Goddesses

If we are what we eat
then eat
like a wild animal

because, baby
my claws & your fangs
make a dream team

And that's what it takes
to give back enough
to keep taking

from
place in a spirit of
reciprocal appropriation

I
Like these spectacular peaks
of the Silvery San Juans
a mountain paradise

tossed up snakeyes against
the roulette blue of the sky
Telluride

Named for a Roman
earth goddess serving up free drinks
in that profound transconscious

CircusCircus of love
where we & the mushrooms
are one

Art Goodtimes

*[Ed. Note: Attic Greek> "to eat is to make, or do"]

Champignon

Champignon gives way
to champagne yawn.
We sleep, replete.

David Oyster

Mushroom

What did you forget
about the forest floor? Where
it has rained for a thousand years

or more. Maybe all
of the answers
are lying there

in the wet black earth,
where already there is
new life growing,

and the old life dying,
and a patch of mushrooms
that you bend to collect,

the last of the season,
and you fill
your sack

with questions,
each one
delicious.

          Erika Moss Gordon

Whispering

Alice remained looking thoughtfully
at the mushroom for a minute,
trying to make out which were
the two sides of it.
– Lewis Carroll

Mushroom, moist murmur
among roots, you grow laced
with shadow and rain, asking
yourself unadorned secrets.

Airica Parker

Expiation

This poem says *Yes* to dark woods.
Yes to rusts and smuts.
Yes to the maggot wriggling
    through still warm flesh.
Yes to wet rot.
Yes to parasitism.
Yes to the death pale saprophyte.
Yes to bole borers.
Yes to the pileated woodpecker.
Yes to the drip and crawl of slime molds.
Yes to termites.
Yes to blackhelmeted fungi.
Yes to the wet mother gathering it all
    back into herself.
Yes to the towering redwood.

        Tony Alcantara

Soiled Barbie

You've heard about the Soiled Dove,
but what about me –

With my fat tease of cloud-spun hair,
hourglass waist cinched between
melon breasts and heart-shaped ass;

How can I get dirty
when my heels won't even
touch the ground?

Sure, my legs can hinge apart,
but there's nothing feral
down there.
Just painted-on panties
and a past-tense pussy
numb as lead;

So, I've learned to talk dirty instead...

Let me be slack-kneed slutty smutty
Let me dream in a shaft that's filled with mold
Let me be dank
Let me be moist
Let me breed crickets and worms in the cold

Let me be nasty germy grimy
Let me fester with raunchy spawn
Let me be fecund
Let me be fetid
Let me itch and squirm and sweat and squat

Oh god, Let me rot!
Let maggots swim
in this shit-soup of darkling
mushroom thoughts
oozing with rancid plastic spots.

     Samantha Tisdel Wright

Foray

the earth itself is fruiting
and the dark longing you keep
locked until august fingers through you like fibrous

webbing. look how your relationship
with truth strains
against the stronger pull of subterranean logic.
see how

even your posture changes;
the sky becomes superfluous.
in the periphery, evidence of the usual chronology:

filling the car with gas, making toast,
making love with
passion or with none. this penumbra
fades into stands

of spruce and aspen, the space
between greens almost holy.
you could crouch here forever, digging tenderly

at the crown of a head. russet, damp with birth,
the surface world's time slowing
to the speed of a heartbeat.

Jennifer Rane Hancock

Walk Slowly

walk slowly with others in the woods
two baskets, a knife, and a brush
look for anything that is not a little brown one
show it off

ask a mushroom if radiation -
vagina lollipops for thirty days -
is a good idea
get some magic help

we want to believe -
like you and the surgeon believe -
he will cut away the sudden sickness
and you will return as if a tourist

sitting, glass of wine at the inn
without a worry
like a bird
like wind in your trees

Rachelle Woods

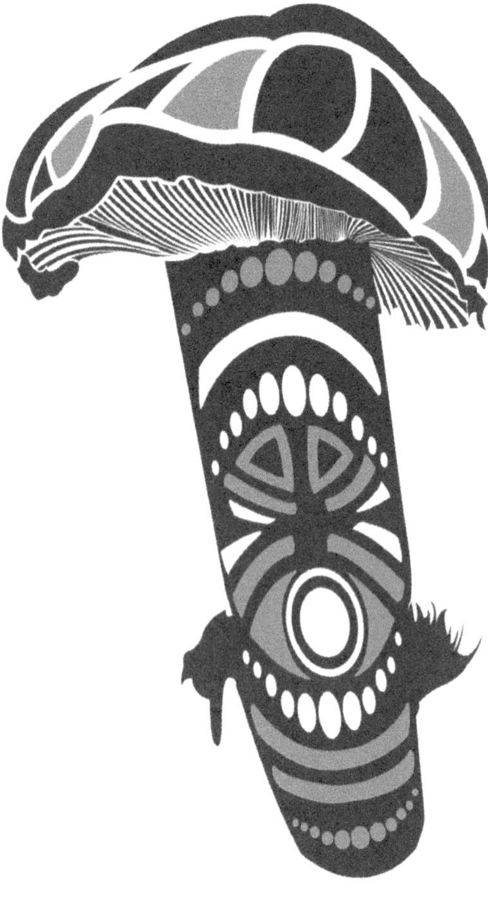

Absorbed

On today, of all days
I found myself
In a Zen garden

Somewhere between here
and there
I sat on the wooden bridge
next to the undulating designs

The pebbles danced
like pebbles will
I glanced at the spotted
caps around my feet

They pointed at the shimmering
sky, a pristine Sistine
In this solitude, I am whole

Nathaniel Kelley

Of Breasts and Mushrooms

A loose jowled, broad shouldered woman
in black wanders our camp
with large handled basket
and pendulous breasts swinging freely
beneath peasant blouse above thin legs.
She asks in lilting accent, perhaps French,
"May I have your mushrooms?"
as though they were ours only for camping for a
price on a mountain where air hums
with RV generator songs.
Admiring her trespass of parceled campground
boundaries, her astute respect for American
habits of possession in a quest for fungal
delicacies, and having enough delighted
in their frumpy company peeking at my pointing
children from tiny mosses and pine duff,
I say, "Yes, of course," and notice her basket
nearly full, soil clinging to creamy sponge roots
below dozens of burnt red waxen caps,
echoing her own robust form.

She squats and pulls. Wanders.
Squats and pulls some more, looks up at me,
around me, as I write. I want to walk with her,
watch her cook these mysteries over fire,
taste her Rocky Mountain dreams
of French cuisine.
I imagine, instead, her crossing into other camps,
ambassador, visiting my rough brothers-in-law,
their blonde wives, leaning against red trucks
and silver mini vans, not far from here,
through lodge pole pines, her gentle request,
their eyes upon her passing swaying breasts,
crude comments chuckled beneath beer breath,
relieved their own wives' tits are tucked away,
firmly compressed, hiding their age,
padded and wired from wandering eyes,
mushrooms unable to rise,
no nipples greeting the duff of day.

Rachel Kellum

Опята [Opjata]

a coppery late September afternoon
hazy with smoke and time
crunching leaves underfoot
plastic bucket lazily swinging from her elbow's crook
Irina leaves the dacha for the still woods
her feet follow the narrow twisting path,
wend their way to the clearing
black and white birches dance a slow supple shuffle
in the crisp autumn breeze,
spectate and screen as she begins her search
nestled in the dank decay and tumbled stumps
the sticky honey mushrooms thrust out their caps
their partial veils rupture without a sound
thumping them into the bucket,
she turns her head at the snapping branch
marking his approach,
the real object of her desire
this smoldering afternoon
eventually the shadows lengthen

luciferase catalyzes luciferin and
foxfire begins to bloom
she gathers up each soul-filled earthen morsel,
parts ways,
traces her steps back home
years later in her Soviet bloc apartment
cluttered with the vague oppressive gray
of primus and Bulgakov,
newspapers line every flat surface -
the fruits of the forest lie scattered everywhere:
berries and fungus dessicating and intensifying,
the countryside lovingly transported to Москва
"I recall all my boyfriends with whom I collected
mushrooms," she confides.
"It is a romantic experience."
But these days, she closes, with brisk economy,
"I hunger for it no more."

     Erin Robertson

The Mushroom

The mushroom is
a reaper,
a healer
and a sage;
as such,
        it labors
ever close to earth,
flourishes
in poverty,
and rarely is taken
seriously.

  Wendy Videlock

Fruiting Bodies

Two Glamdun mushrooms
on the table at Ye Olde
Curiosity Shoppe and Lucas
the proprietor
not a show off
placed one atop
his head and the plumage
rose out of the crown
then a man with no interest
in fungi walked in
and expounded
about the Glamdun's
rarity how they had
even dropped out
of legend
and how this event
two Glamduns
one in plumage
wouldn't happen again
so it was time to die
he skipped out
we all waited
to see the car
strike but
it swerved
death must be
on the other side

        Peter Waldor

Center of the Paradox

Thalia, Muse of Comedy, unfolds
like a school of fish, prods polarity, builds
fences, meets wild stars, sifts
through mist, fog, sun dogs.
Cradled in companionship, interstice
of needles and trees, he inspires beyond genius,

Egypt's hand reaches through a wall,
rubied finger points a revenge warning -
future first born pay backs.
The crossroads' epicenter,
stillness, timeless, tendrils spin out
burst first into fire, next into nothingness.
Dear e. e., nothing is nothing, any time, any place.

St. Frances to the west, Spring Midori to the East.
Feathered arms hug rocks with stone heads, sun
hard surfaces grab fickle wetness, grow moss.
Flat head mushrooms hold moisture in a central
divot on plattered tops. Yellow clover imitates
penstemon, purple imitates thistle.

Paintings and photographs fall from sky,
try to form into sculpture, insist
on imaginary demarcations above
and beneath a pedestal cloud.
They recognize only themselves,
entities of an in-between realm.

Boundaries are complex moving lines
between here now, then there,
you me, them us,
water air, earth fire,
cup spoon, lungs heart,
past future,
red purple blue green yellow orange red.

Patient books wait to be read, know it takes
as long as it takes. One man writes over, erases
another. A crunched soul shoved in a crevice
of his cortex, like a defunct water heater trying
to become a tree. Hard outsides fill with pointed
crystal, delicate on the path to an inside
sacred circle.

False gods claim, *Heretical women burn with lust,*
are prey for The Horsemen. Thalia knows,
Men who take themselves too seriously
are the first to go.

Debbi Brody

Spent Mushroom's Lament

dry & featherlight
the pale yellow edges of my skin curled to a
scalloped sine wave
here on the hot split brown points of pine needles
I find my last repose
a mush room
a toad's stool
a garnish
a side dish
a fairy's wish ringed me in a circle
mycelium
now atrophied, wasted away
I, once the keeper of the word
mycorrhizae
now lie
lighter than wind
uprooted & overturned
with the casual despair of styrofoam
When will the coneys waltz with me once more?
When will the nymphs of Upper Storm Lake
again sing the *Chanson dans la nuit* for me?
"blueberry huckleberry pie" chord
after the rounding of sound boards
the passing of time in irregular rhythms
the fun guy
passes like weathered bone
alone

Erin Robertson

Of Sadness

The mushrooms lull beneath the earth, bald fruit
Of twilight under-trees nuzzling the dark
Like blind moles. And then the rain, frost, seasonal
Shadows, and the mushrooms come muscling

Out like turbaned primitives bearing our old
Farewells, those end stops in the flux, buried,
So achingly remote . . . The mushrooms come
To live, to spore, to die, unloved, unlovely–

Brief determinants of our light air.

Kathryn Winograd

Mushroom Has Landed

Expressionless visitor who appears overnight,
seamless as a spaceship,
neither animal nor vegetable,
your unearthly flesh-likeness, rooted nowhere.

Despite your independence,
you proliferate in our wastes and rot,
play temporary citadel among shadows,
but still submit to our sauté pans,

And bathe just as easily in butter
as in moonlight, donning or losing
your hat for every culinary occasion,
formal or otherwise.

Depending on generation or hemisphere,
you become the handpicked delicacy,
fodder for foodie gossips,
as you sneak unobtrusively with flavor among
wild rice,

Accept the crown as cream of soups,
or stuff yourself endlessly on an entourage of
high-priced hangers-on
among a tray of luxuriant hors d'oeuvres.

Just as you achieve superfood status,
you blanche at the thought of mistaken identity,
of taking blame when your poisonous cousins
the toadstools, mimic you,

force you to return to the woods for respite,
until you pop into fashion again,
but for now, head skyward, shoulders low,
hoping to be beamed up,
before farmer's foot crushes you in the dark.

Cynthia Gallaher

Autumn in Five Parts

    1.

In early autumn, sunny gusts signal a shift,
    the kind of mystery neighborhood crows
    warn about.
In the garden, the last zucchini lies down with the
    cucumber, under an enormous frond.
In its corner, the pumpkin drinks and fattens,
    drinks and fattens, While hailstones pock its
    holes of memory.
Seeds of armyworms under curled leaves
    of baby kale carry more futures than remains.

    2.

Across the street, my neighbor cranks a long
    piece of metal under the hood of his pickup.
For years, he's never spoken or waved or made
    eye contact, except last January first,
    when he was shoveling snow.
At the moment he stood to catch his breath,
    I shouted *Happy New Year* and he lifted
    his hand, kept shoveling.
This time, sunlight catches a long filament flying
    from the eave of his house.
    Now is time for serious work.

3.

Drops of water light on silvery cobwebs stretched
    across mushrooms to blades of grass to
    mushrooms to blades of grass.
A slow bee probes the yellow mum in the terracotta
    planter just the size and shape of a rabbit.
    The wind rises.
My mind rakes the ground under the tall ash while
    the leaves continue to fall one by one,
    as we do.
A single crow slides in and out of view.

4.

How like spiders we are, we aging ladies refusing
    to go gently, grabbing at the forearms
    of our bossy daughters,
We smile at the neighbors and stomp our feet
    at doctors,
We are planning our escapes—one will take a bus
    to Dallas and see what happens.
One will find the now grown child lost
    so many years ago, and one of us thinks
    she will stay put.

5.
Last week, the tangle of planet, sun, and the
 evenness of days
 Aligned as they should.
 Now they begin to unravel.
Yesterday when I opened the garage to grab
 the rake, a six-sided spider web
 filled the doorway .
When I stepped in, the web snapped. I felt the force
 of it against my forehead.
I heard the sound of the trap.

                    Jacqueline St. Joan

Cause and Effect

If I wind up my hand
it will play a song. No, listen,
if I get down on my knees
and beg, if underneath the ferns
there are insects with voices,
some big-celled argument
comes true. Behind the grimace
in cold spring the word *romance,*
if I wind up my hand.
A certain cruelty thrives.
Beneath the forest floor spongy
with mushroom-laced spores.
After the canopy of the trees
beings with extra shadows
copy themselves onto trunks
and water. The comb holds
our sex, and the pattern of violence
makes and mocks us.
If I wind up my hand
it will play the tune
you wanted to hear.

                Judith Skillman

Siempre Cantando
Flowers & Shrooms
– for Enesto Cardenal

Yo ando siempre cantando
Make me a god of flowers & shrooms
Strong man. Story man.

The asphalt's thick with dead
oil. I try to walk the edges
Take distance to heart

And let the head dance
on its own, playing tricks
Joking with friends & strangers

I trust. Not the strangers
we meet via TV's pixels
musing on whose beer's better

Or what car totem tie to buy
Cabezos Hablandos preguntun
"Whose war's as smart as ours?"

Makeup's the best mask for
deception & a tai chi posture of peace
can be a pounce in waiting

Some can pretend anything
except what's true, although
most of us can smell truth

What loves suddenly
may be rot taking root
Lipstick on a pig

Is that an argument against
risk? Have you not been
dissed, diced & duly distracted

by the unexpected razz-a-ma-tazz?
The turquoise blue waterfalls
of Havasupai?

When I was young, I rode
my bike, whistling and making
up songs, willy-nilly

Lyrics to charm the jacaranda
Tame the passionflower
twined around my porch

Time again to make peace our mantra
Make love & celebrate being
so gratefully, about-to-be-dead

alive, & living it up...
So make me one. *Quiero andar*
siempre cantando

Let me find the goddess within
this entangled multiverse
of flowers & shrooms

Art Goodtimes

Everyone Has More Rules Than I Do

like the woman asking to be kissed
by the curling of her hair around
one bare finger. It is nice not to
ask for things but to get them
anyway. I was walking in the woods
and came upon a mushroom monstrous
like the sea. I pressed my fingers against
its spongy side to better see the color
of my red nails that exist that way because
I like the contrast to my white Macbook Pro.
I type as the sky turns over
exposing its whiter side crisp not burned
the way I like bacon. The way the Groomer
keeps giving my dog a schnauzer cut
bothers me. I wonder what they are doing
in the White House right now.
Doodling on white pads of paper
imagining drones striking Syria. Seriously
what *are* the rules of engagement? Everyone
is getting married and everything
is getting farther away.

Holly Coddington

Stony Road

I sat by the road before the storm
Hit, nursing on a pair of gloves, broken

And dreaming the wealth of maples
Crowded in the air above me.

And below, dirt and shade of the street,
Full of noise, and a black-robed woman

With a black umbrella, who turned
And walked toward Law offices, aromas

Of roasting ox. Chickens in her prayers,
A reverence for food, for all things

Slain for our stomachs, praying for health,
And mercy for devouring His creatures.

Give us thy daily bread, oh Lord, and
A mushroom to protect us from Vice,

Dismantled and moved like a circus
To a distant, unnamed watering hole

On the long, stony road before us.

    Alan Basting

The Uses of Speech
(after Magritte, The Uses of Speech Triptych, 1928)

There we are still, hand in hand
at the Brussels Museum,
background in someone's vacation
shots: you, transfixed: *nuage, cheval,
chaussee, fusil...* me,
baffled: *cloud, horse, road, gun...*catching on
to that earthbound *horizon*
like it was the last familiar thing I'd see, the last
of the old country, the one with both of us in it.

Me, hungry for color, texture, globs of paint
piled up on canvas
like mushrooms wet and ripe against the forest floor.
You, satisfied with words, and dry ones.
four masculine, one feminine, a pleasing ratio.
Charcoal on paper, shadow and light.

I'd gather those mushrooms, add wine and broth,
carrots – a chicken if I felt up to wringing
its feathered neck -
and serve a stew of equal parts sustenance,
hallucination, death.
We take our chances, don't we?
You'd crush them, kneeling to brush dust from a rock,
that we might sit awhile.
That we might reconsider, soberly,
before moving on.
Cloud, horse, road, gun.
Horizon.

                Anna Scotti

Myco-Solstice

Unearthing the dark's
shroom shadows
In flickerlight's ember nebulas

And watching stars
like petri dishes of
expanding mycelial thought

Art Goodtimes

Hard (Mushroom)

Rough funguses do protrude the surface—
heavenly yeast of vegetation,
vertical exotic strokes, omnipotent,
tails precluding,
hard-sweet in front of a courtyard
chaise, roughly standing before campers,
drafting matter,
nudge-fruit, center-point.
Bluff rock-rolled rather up,
devil-ish of gray,
many handsome fruits turned soiled.
Your brown spots smitten under fire.
The previous, tighter,
plucks on or for many years
you are an entertainer
and when you know a republic,
a fake empire vanished,
a start, a journey—the means provided
for warmth and illumination.

Ann Huang

Mycelial Mind

Nothing's sustainable about the earth
or our explosive nuclear sun
Who could stop Einstein

from making gravity bend time?
Resilience is no protection
against the terrorists of change

I get National Geo
I've seen the Seven Billion maps
The Nine Billion projections

What curious George
wouldn't want to split the atom?
Spray DDT in the backyard?

Test our trust
in the completely untried?
It's in our evolutionary nature

To experiment. To play at love
& war. We carry within our gills
the spores of our own demise

It's nature's evolutionary failsafe
Taking a species to crash
when it overruns its own good

Keeping Gaia's core molten
whatever surface extinctions
may be spinning our way

Art Goodtimes

Author Bios and Acknowledgments

All poems published herein were first published in *FUNGI* (or soon will be) unless otherwise noted.

Art Goodtimes's poems have appeared in the *Telluride Times-Journal*, the *Telluride Daily Planet*, the *Telluride Watch*, the *Four Corners Free Press* and in his books *As If the World Really Mattered* (2006, La Alameda Press, Albuquerque) and *Looking South to Lone Cone* (2013, Western Eye Press, Sedona).

Airica Parker's works appear in *Camas* (Driftwood Press), and *CALYX*. An accomplished performer, instructor, and healer, Airica makes her home in Colorado. Learn more at airicaparker.com.

Alan Basting was born in Detroit in 1949. He earned an M.A. in English/Creative Writing at Colorado State University and a M.F.A. from Bowling Green State University. His chapbooks include *Singing from the Abdomen* (Stone-Marrow Press), *What the Barns Breathe* (Windows Press), *Suddenly, Herons* (The Writers' Cooperative of Toledo), and *Deep Time, Daily Habits and Events* (from The Arts Commission of Toledo, Ohio). His most recent collection is *Nothing Very Sudden Happens Here* (2013, Lynx House Press, Spokane, WA). He lives in the heart of the Manistee National Forest near the village of Bitely, MI, with his spouse and two dogs.

Amber Veverka is a Charlotte, North Carolina-based freelance writer and editor. She also is a certified environmental educator and master naturalist.

Anna Scotti is a writer, editor, teacher and public speaker living in Southern California. She was recently awarded the Orlando Prize for Short Fiction (AROHO) and the Pocataligo Prize for Poetry (*Yemassee*), and has been nominated for the Pushcart Prize twice. Her work was selected for Best of Ohio 2014, and appears in recent issues of *The Comstock Review*, *Chautauqua*, *Crab Creek Review*, and *The Los Angeles Review*. Much of Scotti's work can be found at annakscotti.com.

Art Beck is currently at work translating a large selection of the, 1st century c.e. epigrammist, Martial, for a volume potentially entitled *Mea Roma*.

Beth Paulson lives in Ridgway, Colorado where she teaches writing classes, leads Poetica, a monthly workshop for area writers, and co-directs the Open Bard Poetry Series. Her poems have appeared nationally in over a hundred journals and anthologies and she has received three Pushcart Prize nominations. Her newest book, *Canyon Notes*, was published in 2012 by Mt. Sneffels Press. "Chanterelles" originally appeared in *Wild Raspberries* (2009, Plain View Press).

A resident of California's Mendocino Coast, Blake More is an artist with multiple creative voices and obsessions. Blurring the boundaries between disciplines, her work includes poetry, video, radio, performance, costume design, collage, teaching, painting, functional mixed media art/life pieces and wildly painted poetry art cars, including her newest, Star Yantra (staryantra.life). She hosts two radios shows, a web radio show called "Cartwheels on the Sky" and Women's Voices on KZYX&Z Mendocino. Her book *godmeat* is a collection of poetry, prose, color artwork, and a DVD compilation of poem movies (available at godmeat.com), and her latest chapbook *Up In the Me World* is available on her website. To explore more of Blake's creative world, please visit snakelyone.com.

Blaize Johnson lives in a cargo shipping container, somewhere between the jungle and the ocean. She spends most of the day photographing waves breaking, and birds in flight. For several years she has simply written "poet" as her occupation on customs forms; it seems to be going okay.

Carol Anne Modena was born and grew up in Westfield, Massachusetts, where her only relationship with mushrooms was Campbell's Cream of Mushroom Soup. She spent her professional life in New York State as a teacher and educational administrator. During that time she created and launched a statewide program to train day care workers. She retired to Port Townsend, Washington where she now lives on the edge of the Salish Sea with her husband Jim. She is an avid gardener, vegetarian cook, recovering fungophobic, and a poetry student at The Writers' Workshoppe.

CB Follett is the author of 11 poetry books, most recently *NOAH'S BOAT* (2016) and several chapbooks. She has numerous nominations for Pushcart Prizes, both as an individual poet and for particular poems. She was awarded a Marin Arts Council Grant for Poetry, and is widely published nationally and internationally. Follett served as Marin County Poet Laureate from 2010-2013. "Iron County" first appeared in the book *Visible Bones* by CB Follett.

Cynthia Gallaher, a Chicago-based poet, playwright and nonfiction writer, is author of three full poetry collections, *Earth Elegance*, *Swimmer's Prayer* and *Night Ribbons*. Her most recent chapbook is *Omnivore Odes: Poems About Food, Herbs and Spices*. The Chicago Public Library lists her among its "Top Ten Requested Chicago Poets." Most recently, she published a nonfiction reference/memoir *Frugal Poets' Guide to Life: How to Live a Poetic Life, Even If You Aren't a Poet*. "Mushroom Has Landed" first appeared in *FUNGI*, and soon after was included in the chapbook *Omnivore Odes: Poems About Food, Herbs and Spices* (2013, Finishing Line Press).

David Feela, a retired teacher, poet, free-lance writer, and workshop instructor, resides in Arriola, Colorado. His chapbook, *Thought Experiments* (Maverick Press), won the Southwest Poet Series, and a full length poetry collection, *The Home Atlas* (2009, WordTech Editions), is available online. A collection of essays, *How Delicate These Arches* (2011, Raven's Eye Press), was chosen as a finalist for the Colorado Book Award. His web site is feelasophy.weebly.com. "Shameless" appeared in a previous publication, an online journal: SageGreenJournal.org.

Debbi Brody is an avid attendee and leader of poetry workshops throughout the Southwest. She has been published in numerous national and regional journals, magazines and anthologies of note. Her newest full length poetry book, *In Everything, Birds* (2015, Village Books Press, OKC, OK), is available at independent bookstores across the US, through the author at artqueen58@aol.com and at the usual on-line purchase sites.

Donald Levering's latest book, *Coltrane's God*, published by Red Mountain Press, won the New Mexico Press Women Poetry Book Contest in 2016. His previous book, *The Water Leveling with Us*, placed 2nd in the 2015 National Federation of Press Women Creative Verse Book Competition. Levering won the 2014 Literal Latté Award and was 1st Runner-Up for the Mark Fischer Prize in 2015 and was a Runner-Up for the 2016 Ruth Stone Poetry Prize. He lives in Santa Fe, New Mexico. "The Kingdom of Ignorance" was first published by *The Maryland Poetry Review*. It also was the title poem of a chapbook from Finishing Line Press.

Elle Masaracchia is a poet and novelist, as well as an English teacher, in Southern California. She has written over 300 poems since 2012 and published her first novel, *Nautilus*, in 2014. She is currently working on 3 separate novels and continues to write poetry daily. Elle hopes to create new pathways for understanding, both humanity and the world we live in, through her literary work. For poetry and short stories, or to order her book, please see www.ellemasaracchia.com.

Erika Moss Gordon lives in the mountains of southwest Colorado where she writes poetry, works for a film festival and teaches yoga. Erika's writing has appeared in *Mountain Gazette Magazine*, *FUNGI*, *Telluride Watch*, *Telluride Magazine*, *Telluride Inside and Out*, *Grand Junction Daily Sentinel*, *Salmonberry Arts* and *99 Poems for the 99 Percent*, a collection of poetry. Her most recent book, *Phases*, was winner of the Fledge Chapbook Award, published by Middle Creek Publishing in 2016. Her first chapbook, *Of Eyes and Iris*, was published in 2013 (Liquid Light Press). "Mushroom" appears in *Phases* (2016, Middle Creek Publishing and Audio).

Erin Robertson lives in Louisville, Colorado and writes in the quiet dark hours when the house goes to sleep. A biologist by training, she finds ways to weave her love of words and the natural world. Visit erinrobertson.org for more.

Haz Said lives in Pagosa Springs, Colorado. "The Risen" first appeared in *Arborglyph*, a chapbook for the National Forest Service.

Henri Bensussen writes about her world as a way to understand it while she is still living it. Her first poetry chapbook, *Earning Colors*, was published in 2015 by Finishing Line Press. She earned a BA in Biology at the University of California, Santa Cruz, where she studied fungi but did not eat them. "Root to Hyphal Rootlet" is based on an unexpected encounter with a man gathering chanterelles. In that Douglas-fir forest near the Oregon coast, she became an intruder of his private hunting grounds, as he became an intruder into her solitary existence.

Jacqueline St. Joan writes fiction, nonfiction and poetry. She has won numerous poetry awards and has been published in a wide variety of periodicals. Her first book of poems, *What Remains*, is forthcoming from Turkey Buzzard Press. *My Sisters Made of Light*, her first novel, was a finalist for the 2011 Colorado Book Award in Literary Fiction. She is coeditor of *Beyond Portia: Women, Law, and Literature in the United States*. She lives in Denver where she serves as Ziggies Poet of the Year. She can be found at mysistersmadeoflight.com.

Jeanetta Calhoun Mish's "Ode to Psilocybe" was first published in *What I Learned at the War* (2016, West End Press). She can be found at tonguetiedwoman.com.

Jennifer Rane Hancock received her MFA from Sarah Lawrence College, and her PhD from Oklahoma State University. She is currently Assistant Professor of English at Colorado Mesa University, and her first collection is *Between Hurricanes* (2015, Lithic Press). Her work has also appeared in *Ecotone*, *Crab Orchard Poetry Review*, and *Puerto del Sol*, among other journals. She occasionally forays on the Grand Mesa, where sadly someone else has found her chanterelle field.

Jose A. Alcantara is a father and math teacher who lives in western Colorado. His poems have appeared in *The Midwest Quarterly*, *Spoon River Poetry Review*, *Palimpsest*, and *99 Poems for the 99%*. He was a 2013 Fishtrap Fellow in Poetry.

Judith Skillman's recent book is *House of Burnt Offerings* (Pleasure Boat Studio). Awards include an Eric Mathieu King Fund grant from the Academy of American Poets for *Storm*, Blue Begonia Press. Visit her at judithskillman.com. "Cause and Effect" appears in *Angles of Separation* (Glass Lyre Press).

Judyth Hill, poet, author, editor, writing teacher, lives in the magnificent aspen-swept mountains of northern Colorado. Judyth conducts poetry workshops at writing conferences internationally, is an annual Poet-in-Residence at schools in the United States, offers writing classes online at judythhill.com, and on-going classes in San Miguel de Allende in Mexico. She leads WildWriting Culinary Adventures around the world, eat-write-travel.com. Her nine published books of poetry include *Men Need Space*, *Dazzling Wobble* and *Tzimzum*. Her newest book, *Love Called Me Here*, is forthcoming in 2018. She is the author of the internationally acclaimed poem,

"Wage Peace," published around the world; set to music, performed and recorded by national choirs and orchestras.

Kathryn Winograd is the author of *Phantom Canyon: Essays of Reclamation*, a Foreward Reviews' Book of the Year Award Finalist, and *Air into Breath*, a Colorado Book Award Winner in Poetry. Visit her at kathrynwinograd.com.

Lynda La Rocca is a freelance writer and poet who lives in Twin Lakes, Colorado. Her poetry books include *The Stillness Between* (2009, Pudding House Publications, Ohio) and *Spiral* (2012, Liquid Light Press, Colorado). Lynda loves writing, reading, cooking (and eating), hiking, birding, nature, performing (since 2004) with the performance-poetry troupe the River City Nomads, and most of all, her husband Steve Voynick and their dog Luz and turtle SunSpot.

Nathaniel Kelley currently lives in Chicago. He is finishing his first book of poetry, essays and photography.

Peter Waldor is the author of four books of poetry, including *Who Touches Everything*, which won the National Jewish Book Award for poetry.

Rachel Kellum shares a prairie with her family, a herd of red heifers, two pigs and nine chickens on the eastern plains of Colorado. She teaches writing, literature, humanities and art at Morgan Community College where she also serves as director of the CACE Gallery of Fine Art and hosts Open Mic Poetry Nights. She is a founding member of Tumbleweed Poets, a local chapter of Colorado's state poetry society. A Pushcart Prize nominee and NFSPS award winning poet, Kellum's poetry has been featured in several online journals and in the international collection, Lush. Kellum leads writing workshops, performs her poetry around Colorado and blogs at wordweeds.com. Her first book, *ah*, published by Liquid Light Press, was released in 2012. "Of Breasts and Mushrooms," was first published in *Four Corners Free Press* (2011).

Rachel Woods's poem "Walk Slowly" first published in Adobe Walls (2012).

Robert Michael Pyle dwells, writes, and studies natural history in the Lower Columbia watershed. His twenty books include *Wintergreen* (winner of the John Burroughs Medal), *Sky Time in Gray's River*, *The Thunder Tree*, *The Tangled Bank*, *Evolution of the Genus Iris*; *Poems*, *Chinook & Chanterelle: Poems*, and a flight of butterfly books. Bob has taught place-based writing at Utah State University, as Kittredge Distinguished Writer at the University of Montana, and from Tasmania to Tajikistan. He is currently making poems and music with his friend, neighbor, and Grange brother, Nirvana bassist Krist Novoselic. "Chinook & Chanterelle" was originally published as a broadside by The PeasandCues Press, Longview, Washington. Subsequently it appeared in *Northwest Coast Magazine*, and in the anthology

Decomposition (eds. Renée Roehl & Kelly Chadwick) and the book *Chinook & Chanterelle: Poems* by Robert Michael Pyle, both published by Lost Horse Press.

Rosemerry Wahtola Trommer was appointed Colorado's Western Slope Poet Laureate (2015-2017). Favorite mushroom: Morel. Favorite one-word mantra: Adjust. Visit her at wordwoman.com.

Roy Beckemeyer is from Wichita, Kansas. His poems have recently appeared in *The Midwest Quarterly*, *Kansas City Voices*, *The North Dakota Review*, *Dappled Things*, and *I-70 Review*. Two of his poems were nominated for the 2016 Pushcart Prize competition. His debut collection of poetry, *Music I Once Could Dance To* (2014, Coal City Press), was selected as a 2015 Kansas Notable Book.

Independent journalist and poet Samantha Tisdel Wright lives and writes amidst the San Juan Mountains of southwestern Colorado, where she's on the lookout for the next great patch of chanterelles.

A retired middle-school English teacher, Suzanne Rogier Marshall has published professional articles, poetry, and a book on teaching writing. Her poems have appeared recently or are forthcoming in *Tinderbox Poetry Journal*, *Smoky Quartz*, *The Tule Review*, *Written River*, and *Freshwater* as well as other journals and anthologies. Her first chapbook *Blood Knot* was released in June 2015 (Porkbelly Press). Suzanne lives with her husband in the mountains of New Hampshire, where she draws inspiration for her writing.

Wendy Videlock is a poet, teacher, and visual artist living in Palisade, Colorado. Her work has appeared in *Poetry Magazine*, *The New Criterion*, *Dark Horse*, *Rattle*, and other literary journals. Her books (*Nevertheless*, *The Dark Gnu*, and *Slingshots*) are available from Able Muse Press. Wendy's visual art can be found in galleries throughout the Western Slope. To see more of Wendy's work please visit: http://nutshell-wendy.blogspot.com.

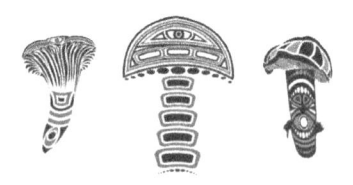